FORENSIC FILE

THE MURDER MANUAL OF A TEENAGE KILLER

Kemi Adeyoola's Plan to Make Millions by Murder

by Edward Nicholson

Prison and After: Making Life Count

Copyright © ticktock Entertainment Ltd 2007

First published in Great Britain in 2007 by ticktock Media Ltd,
2 Orchard Business Centre, North Farm Road, Tunbridge Wells, Kent, TN2 3XF

ticktock project editor: Joe Harris
ticktock project designer: Hayley Terry
Series consultant: Dr John P Cassella

ISBN: 978 1 84696 510 4 pbk

Printed in China

Picture credits (t=top; b=bottom; c=centre; l=left; r=right; OBC=outside back cover;
OFC=outside front cover): Alamy: (SHOUT) 12b, (Don Smetzer) 13cr, (Arthur Turner)18b,
Simon Rawles) 22b. Anglia Press Agency: 11tr. Arrestingimages.com/ Mikael Karlsson: 8tl,
12t, 17c. brandXpictures: OBCb, 19b, 25b, 27r. iStockphoto: (Carmen Martínez Banús) 13tl,
(Lisa Kyle Young)15b, (Joe Gough)20b, (Pascal Genest)21b, (David Playford)24, 27l. PA
Photos/Andrew Parsons/PA Archive: 4cr, 22t, 26t. Rex Features: OBCt, 5b, 6t 6b (Ben
Granville), 7bl (Ben Dome), 8br,10 (Zazou), 25c (Prescilla Coleman), 26b, 28br. Science
Photo Library: (Michael Donne) 9cr, 26c. Shutterstock: OFC, 1, 2, 3, 4bl, 5tr, 5tl, 7tr, 7br, 9tr,
11br, 13tr, 14t, 14bl, 15tr, 15c, 16, 17br, 17tr, 18t, 18c, 19tr, 19tl, 20t, 21tr, 21l, 23, 25tr, 28bl,
29. Superstock: (Charles Orrico) 9br, (fStop) 30. ticktock Media Archive: 4t, 11tl,14br.

Contents

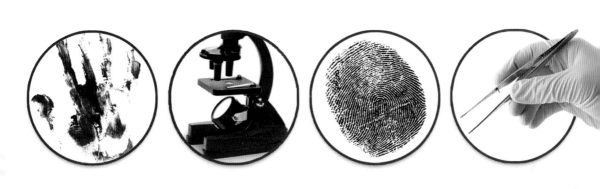

A Shocking Sight

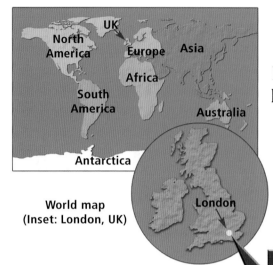

World map
(Inset: London, UK)

To Leonard and Anne Mendel, a retired couple living peacefully in the north London suburb of Golders Green, 14th March 2005 seemed just an ordinary day. Little did they realise that a dangerous criminal had terrible plans for them.

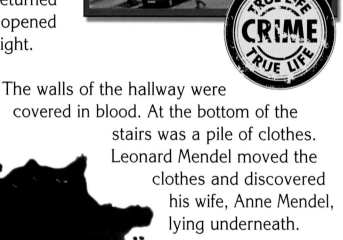

Elmcroft Crescent

Leonard Mendel left their home at 9.45am to pick up some plane tickets from the nearby travel agent's. He and Anne were planning to visit their daughter in Israel. He returned home at 11.00am and opened the door to a horrible sight.

TRUE LIFE
CRIME
TRUE LIFE

The walls of the hallway were covered in blood. At the bottom of the stairs was a pile of clothes. Leonard Mendel moved the clothes and discovered his wife, Anne Mendel, lying underneath.

Leonard Mendel wasn't sure if Anne was alive or dead. He tried to call for an ambulance but found that the phone line had been cut.

The murderer had cut through the phone line in the hall.

FORENSIC FACTFILE
A Vicious Murder

Victim   **Age**
Anne Mendel   85

Marital Status
Married to Leonard Mendel, 81

Date of Murder
14th March 2005

Crime Scene
The home of Anne and Leonard Mendel on Elmcroft Crescent, in Golders Green, London, UK.

Time of Death
Between 9.45am and 11.00am

Murder victim Anne Mendel.

Cause of Death

The phone line in the hallway had been cut, but Leonard Mendel found that the phone in the kitchen was still working. He dialled 999 and asked for an ambulance.

Leonard Mendel gave his wife **mouth-to-mouth resuscitation** (the kiss of life) until the ambulance arrived. At 11.30am, the police were called – Anne Mendel was dead.

Forensic teams searched the **crime scene** for clues. They found that the lock on the front door had not been forced. This suggested that Anne Mendel had known her attacker, and had let them into her home.

The police interviewed Leonard Mendel. They decided he was not a murder suspect.

Anne Mendel's body was taken to Finchley **Mortuary**, north London, for a **post-mortem**. A **forensic pathologist** examined the body and found the cause of death was stab wounds to the chest. Anne Mendel had been stabbed 14 times.

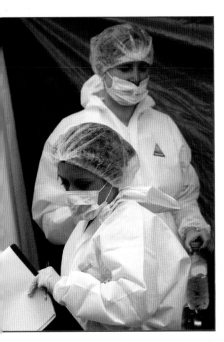

Forensic investigators searched Anne and Leonard Mendel's house for evidence.

A Killer on the Loose

Before removing Anne Mendel's body from the murder scene, the forensic team working on the case had checked it for evidence. They hoped that the killer could be traced from their **DNA**.

Just one scrap of DNA evidence was found: a small piece of skin, under Anne Mendel's fingernail. This evidence was then checked against a database of the DNA of known criminals.

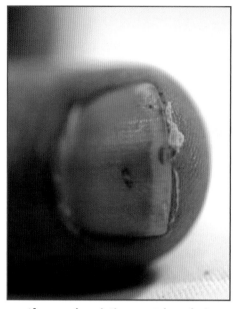

If a murder victim scratches their attacker, DNA evidence may be trapped under their fingernails.

In a typical murder case, forensic scientists compare two samples of DNA – an 'evidence' sample, and a 'reference' sample. In this case the 'evidence' sample was collected from Anne Mendel's hand. The 'reference' samples were held on the DNA database.

The forensic scientists found a match! The DNA evidence found on Anne Mendel belonged to a 16-year-old girl named Kemi Adeyoola.

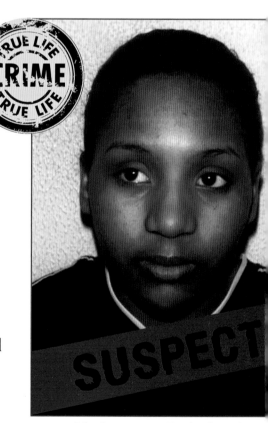

Murder suspect Kemi Adeyoola.

FORENSIC FACTFILE
DNA Testing

- The science of DNA testing has transformed forensic detective work.

- DNA is short for 'deoxyribonucleic acid'. We each carry our own unique DNA combination in the cells of our bodies.

- The police keep a database of the DNA of known criminals. When they find DNA evidence at a crime scene, they check this against their database.

- If the DNA from the crime scene matches the database, that is evidence that the samples probably came from the same person.

A police officer labels DNA samples taken from a suspect.

"The police hoped the killer could be traced from their DNA."

A forensic scientist prepares a DNA sample for testing.

The Prime Suspect

DNA evidence had led detectives straight to Kemi Adeyoola. She was the teenage daughter of a millionaire businessman and former boxer, Bola Adeyoola.

Shoplifting is the most common crime among young women in the UK.

Kemi Adeyoola had been sent to an expensive **boarding school**. After her parents argued over school fees, she moved with her mother to Golders Green in north London. It was at this time that she started getting into trouble.

Kemi Adeyoola offended many neighbours with her **antisocial** behaviour. She had assaulted a neighbour. She also became a regular **shoplifter**.

Kemi Adeyoola was sent to the young offenders' wing at Bullwood Hall Prison, in Essex. She served three months for shoplifting. She had been released from Bullwood Hall only a few months before the murder.

> *" Adeyoola had assaulted a neighbour. "*

Golders Green, North London

Bullwood Hall Prison, Essex

London

English Channel

Map of south-east England, showing Golders Green and Bullwood Hall.

FORENSIC FACTFILE
Young Offenders

- **Young offenders** are criminals aged 10 to 21. They are too young to be sent to an adult prison.

- Between the ages of 15 and 21, they may be imprisoned in special young offenders' institutions, or in young offenders' wings of adult prisons, like Bullwood Hall.

- Young offenders have to obey strict rules while in prison. They receive up to 25 hours of education activities each week to help them.

There are only about 80 female young offenders imprisoned in England and Wales.

Questioning the Suspect

Kemi Adeyoola was arrested on 12th May 2005, and the police questioned her about Anne Mendel's murder. They told her that she had been linked to the crime scene by forensic evidence.

Suspects are handcuffed to stop them escaping from police.

Adeyoola changed her story several times.

Kemi Adeyoola tried to explain why skin with her DNA had been found on Anne Mendel's hand. She said she had been in Golders Green the day before the murder. She had visited Sally's Beauty Supply and bought two 'hair-relaxing' chemical kits.
She said she had met an old lady, Anne Mendel, between 2pm and 4pm on Golders Green Road, by the junction with Finchley Road.

A police officer prepares to interview a suspect.

Kemi Adeyoola claimed she had helped Anne Mendel to cross the road.

Kemi Adeyoola said she held Anne Mendel's hand while she crossed the road. As they crossed, Anne Mendel slipped and scratched the teenager's hand. However Kemi Adeyoola changed her story several times, saying that this meeting had taken place on different days.

FORENSIC FACTFILE
Adeyoola's Lies

The police suspected Kemi Adeyoola was lying for these reasons:

- Sally's Beauty Supply said they did not sell hair-relaxing chemicals.

Kemi Adeyoola lied about visiting this shop.

- A search of Kemi Adeyoola's flat showed she owned no hair-relaxing chemicals, just hair-straightening tongs.

- Anne Mendel's movements from the 12th and 13th March showed it was unlikely she would have been in Golders Green.

- Kemi Adeyoola's mobile phone records showed that on the afternoon of 13th March, she was in the West End. This is a part of central London, far from Golders Green.

Kemi Adeyoola's Alibi

Kemi Adeyoola gave the police an **alibi** for the morning of the murder. She claimed that she had been at a bus garage in Alperton, north-west London.

Was Kemi Adeyoola really looking for her purse when the murder took place?

Kemi Adeyoola said she had been collecting a purse which she had lost on a bus. However, records of calls made from Kemi Adeyoola's phone showed she had actually been near her home in Belsize Park, north London. This was a long way from Alperton, but just a short journey from Golders Green, where Anne Mendel was murdered.

Map of London showing where Kemi Adeyoola claimed to be when the murder took place.

Police were able to trace Kemi Adeyoola's movements using her phone records.

FORENSIC FACTFILE
Mobile Phone Records

- Police can track suspected criminals through their use of mobile phones.

- Mobiles cannot show exactly where they were used, but they communicate through **base stations**.

- Police can find out which base station a phone user was nearest to, and use that to work out their location.

- Police can also listen to phone conversations or read text messages sent from mobile phones. However, they need the permission of the government to do this.

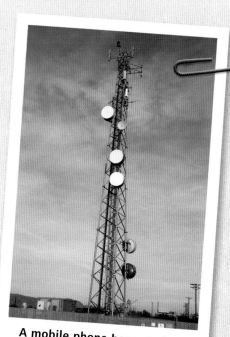

A mobile phone base station.

RECONSTRUCTION

Police had made more discoveries about Kemi Adeyoola's background. She had lived next door to Anne and Leonard Mendel in Golders Green. Anne Mendel had been kind to her. She let Adeyoola stay in her house when she didn't have a key to get into her own home. Had Adeyoola selected her friendly former neighbour as a victim?

Anne Mendel was very trusting. She welcomed Adeyoola into her home when she was locked out.

A Surprising Discovery

The police soon made another breakthrough. They discovered that while Kemi Adeyoola was in prison at Bullwood Hall, she had written a book about killing an elderly woman.

Prison and After: Making Life Count

Young offenders' cells are regularly searched to make sure they aren't hiding anything.

The book was called *Prison and After: Making Life Count*. This 'murder manual' had been found during a **routine cell search**. It was an 18-page, detailed plot describing how she planned to murder a defenceless elderly victim to make £3 million.

When the murder manual was discovered, **forensic psychologist** Lydia Sear questioned Kemi Adeyoola about it. Adeyoola said that it was a crime novel she was writing. She said it was inspired by her love of crime novelists like James Patterson and Martina Cole.

Kemi Adeyoola loved to read novels about murder. However, her manual was more than a just a work of fiction.

FORENSIC FACTFILE
Cell Searches

- The cells of prisoners and young offenders are searched often, but not at regular intervals. It is important that prisoners cannot guess when their rooms are going to be searched.

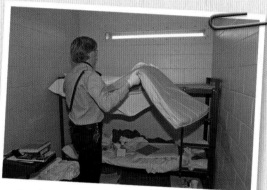

A prison officer performs a cell search.

- During cell searches, prison staff look for drugs and illegal items, and dangerous objects such as knives or scissors.

- Prison staff wear protective gloves while they search.

- They may use special tools to help them with their search, such as long-handled mirrors and hand-held metal detectors.

The Murder Manual

In her murder manual, Kemi Adeyoola laid out her plans for the future. She described how she would buy a home through **fraud** and deception. She also explained how she would get a high-paying job by lying about her academic qualifications and **forging** official documents.

The manual contained a shopping list including butchers' knives, handcuffs, drugs, hoods and stun guns. Adeyoola wrote about buying drugs to cause **memory loss** and **paralysis** in her victim. Her plan was to creep up on and attack an elderly, defenceless victim.

Adeyoola planned to buy tools that could disable and terrify her helpless victim. A stun gun (below) can electrocute a person without killing them.

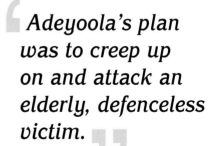

" Adeyoola's plan was to creep up on and attack an elderly, defenceless victim. "

Kemi Adeyoola described how she would torture her victim into revealing their private bank account numbers, and the code to their private **safe**. She could then steal all their money and valuables. She imagined building a 'tent' made of cling-film to catch the victim's blood and wrote about how she would dispose of the body.

Many older people keep their money and other valuables in safes at home.

FORENSIC FACTFILE
Psychological Assessment

- Kemi Adeyoola lied to prison psychologists, saying she had achieved four 'A' grades at GCSE. This led them to report that she was intelligent, and could do well if released.

- Adeyoola prided herself on being a good liar. During an interview with a youth worker she made herself cry and mumble, so that they would feel sorry for her.

- A psychiatric report was prepared on Adeyoola, which said she was unlikely ever to commit violence. Adeyoola had fooled the authorities.

Outwardly, Kemi Adeyoola seemed normal, but secretly she fantasised about violence and cruelty.

Rehearsing the Perfect Murder

Kemi Adeyoola planned to follow a rich, elderly victim home, before killing them.

In her book, Kemi Adeyoola described stalking an elderly woman in a wealthy area. "Run lightly and silently behind her and cover her mouth with a gloved hand," she wrote. "Make her so scared she cooperates."

After Anne Mendel's murder, the police suspected that this document was no work of fiction but a deadly serious plan for murder. But Anne Mendel was not wealthy. Why had Kemi Adeyoola targeted her?

Kemi Adeyoola's goal was to make at least £3 million.

During the trial of Kemi Adeyoola, the **prosecution** argued that the murder of Anne Mendel was a 'trial run'. Kemi Adeyoola was testing her plan to see if it worked, before going on to murder someone wealthy. Clearly she expected to get away with this murder and go on to kill again.

Adeyoola planned to wear gloves during the murder, to hide her fingerprints.

The killing of Anne Mendel was a rehearsal for another murder.

FORENSIC FACTFILE
A Psychopath

Many people investigating the Kemi Adeyoola case believed that she was a psychopath.

- A psychopath is a person who cannot share or understand the feelings of others. Kemi Adeyoola did not seem to care about the misery that she caused the Mendel family.

- Psychopaths are very good liars. Kemi Adeyoola boasted that she had been able to trick a social worker into feeling sorry for her during an interview.

- Psychopaths are extremely selfish. Adeyoola was apparently willing to do anything in her pursuit of £3 million.

Psychopaths may use fear and violence to achieve their selfish goals.

The False Alibi Scheme

Holloway Prison, in north London.

Detectives charged Kemi Adeyoola with the murder of Anne Mendel and held her on **remand** at Holloway Prison in north London. While she was awaiting trial, Kemi Adeyoola began to plot how she would create a fake **alibi** to prove she had not killed Anne Mendel.

Kemi Adeyoola and her sister, Sade, placed an advert in *The Brent Leader* newspaper. The advert asked anyone who had seen Kemi Adeyoola on a bus on the morning of the murder to contact her solicitors.

Holloway is Europe's largest women's prison, and holds 478 prisoners.

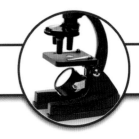

Kemi Adeyoola told Natasha Greenwood, a 16-year-old prisoner, to find a person outside the prison who they could pay to lie. This person would say they had seen Kemi Adeyoola on the 268 bus at the time of the murder.

FORENSIC FACTFILE

Alibis

- To have committed a crime, a suspect must have been in the right place at the right time.

- An alibi is a claim that a suspect was somewhere else when the crime took place. In Latin, 'alibi' means 'elsewhere'.

- Acting as a false alibi witness is a serious crime.

However, Kemi Adeyoola's plan to find a false alibi witness was spoiled by Greenwood. She told the police about the plot, and said she had pretended to go along with the plan to keep Kemi Adeyoola calm.

If she was the murderer, Kemi Adeyoola could not have been on the 268 bus when Anne Mendel was killed.

The Court Case

Kemi Adeyoola's court case began on 6th June 2006. She denied murder. She tried to influence the judge and **jury** by crying and shaking in court when she was questioned.

On 27th June 2006 at the Old Bailey court in London, Kemi Adeyoola, then aged 18, was found guilty of the murder of 85-year-old Anne Mendel. She was also found guilty of trying to deceive the court, by plotting to invent a false alibi.

Judge Richard Hone called her a 'cold-blooded killer who is a danger to the public'.

The statue of Justice at the top of the Old Bailey court.

" You are a cold-blooded killer who is a danger to the public. "

The following day, Kemi Adeyoola was sentenced to life in prison. Speaking outside court, Adeyoola's father disowned her. He described his daughter as a 'monster' and said: "What she did was evil. She is no longer my daughter."

This illustration shows Kemi Adeyoola being questioned. Cameras are not allowed in British courts.

Kemi Adeyoola will be behind bars until at least 2026.

FORENSIC FACTFILE
The Jury

- **Jurors** are usually chosen at random from the adult population. This is known as jury service.

- There are 12 people on jury. They listen to the case and tell the judge whether they believe the accused was 'guilty' or 'not guilty'.

- The jury in the case of Anne Mendel took 23 hours to reach the decision that Kemi Adeyoola was guilty.

Case Closed

14th March 2005

85-year-old Anne Mendel was brutally stabbed to death in her home.

12th May 2005

Kemi Adeyoola was arrested on suspicion of murder after police found a match between her DNA and the DNA on Anne Mendel's hand. She was a known criminal, although her previous crimes had been much less serious.

May 2005 onwards

The police discovered that while Kemi Adeyoola was imprisoned at Bullwood Hall, she had written a murder manual.

In the manual she described how she would kill an old woman. She had also written plans to cheat and lie to get a well-paid job and make herself rich.

Kemi Adeyoola repeatedly lied to the police during interviews. They could tell she was lying by looking at her mobile phone records, by interviewing shopkeepers, and asking Leonard Mendel about his wife's movements.

December 2005

While awaiting trial at Holloway Prison, Kemi Adeyoola tried to find a false alibi witness. She was not successful in this plan, because another prisoner spoke to the police.

6th June 2006

The trial of Kemi Adeyoola began at the Old Bailey Court in London.

27th June 2006

Kemi Adeyoola was found guilty of the murder of Anne Mendel, and of trying to deceive the court.

28th June 2006

Kemi Adeyoola was sentenced to life in prison.

DNA Matching

- DNA is a unique chemical code we each carry in the cells of our bodies. We inherit our DNA from our parents.

- Scientists only need a tiny amount of DNA, such as a drop of blood or a single eyelash, to create a DNA profile which they can read. Various different scientific methods can be used to create a profile.

- When criminals are convicted, the inside of their mouths are scratched with a **swab**. This gives the police a sample of their DNA.

- Information about criminals' DNA is stored on a national computer database.

- When the police have a DNA profile from a crime scene, they compare it to the national computer database. This contains millions of profiles of known criminals.

- The strength of DNA-based proof depends on how unusual the DNA profile is. The more unusual the DNA profile, the more likely it is that it could not be shared by anyone else.

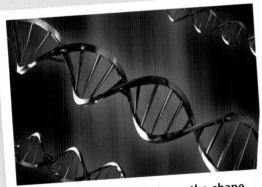

This computer model shows the shape of a DNA molecule.

A forensic scientist studies a DNA profile.

Documentary Evidence

- In the Anne Mendel murder case, the murder manual written by Kemi Adeyoola was one of the main pieces of evidence against the killer.

- When documents are used as evidence in a trial, this is known as documentary evidence. It is usually written or typed documents, but it can involve other media, such as film.

Examples of documentary evidence

- Photographs
- Official documents
- Letters
- Films
- Tape recordings
- Printed emails

- However, sometimes letters or photos are physical evidence. If the contents of a letter are used in court, then it is documentary evidence. But if a blood-stained letter is used to show the angle of a stabbing, then it is physical evidence. In these cases the contents of the letter are not important.

- If documentary evidence supposedly belonged to a criminal, their ownership of the object must first be proved. In Adeyoola's case, the murder manual was found in her cell in a locked institution and was in her handwriting. This proved that she had written it.

A video relating to a crime is another form of documentary evidence.

Letters often contain important documentary evidence.

Forensic Database

Post-mortems

When someone dies in a suspicious or violent way, the police may request a post-mortem. A post-mortem is a medical examination of a dead body. It is used to find out how someone died. The person who carries out the post-mortem is called a **forensic pathologist**.

- The forensic pathologist first examines the outside of the body. Any bruises or wounds are measured and photographed. The body is also x-rayed.

- The pathologist then makes a deep, y-shaped cut in the body's chest. The internal organs are removed one by one. Each organ is weighed and carefully examined.

- If the forensic pathologist suspects that the corpse has been poisoned, they will send samples of the internal organs to a poison expert, called a **toxicologist**.

- The pathologist then cuts open the head, and removes the brain. This is also weighed and examined.

- After the post-mortem, all the organs are returned to the body and it is sewn closed with strong thread.

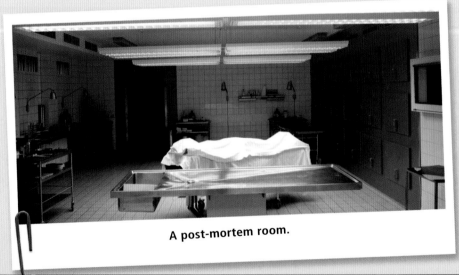

A post-mortem room.

Glossary

alibi: Evidence that proves a suspect could not have been at the crime scene when the crime took place.

antisocial: Unfriendly or aggressive toward other people.

base station: A mast which sends signals to mobile phones.

boarding school: A school where students live as well as study.

cell search: Looking for banned items in a prison cell.

crime scene: An area where evidence of an illegal act is found.

crime scene investigator: Someone who looks for forensic evidence at a crime scene.

DNA: A molecule present in many living cells which gives the instructions for making a plant, animal, or other organism. Each human's DNA is unique, unless they are an identical twin.

forensic: Using science in the investigation of a crime.

forensic pathologist: A doctor who performs post-mortems and is trained to work out how someone died.

forensic psychologist: An expert in scientific evidence to do with the human mind.

forensic scientist: A scientist who examines evidence to do with crimes.

forge: Make a false document.

fraud: Breaking the law by lying, for example in order to make money.

juror: One of the people in a jury.

jury: A group of people who decide whether someone accused of a crime is guilty.

memory loss: Forgetfulness, caused by illness or drugs.

mortuary: A place where dead bodies are kept before they are buried or cremated.

mouth-to-mouth resuscitation: A first aid technique where someone blows air into another person's mouth, to start them breathing.

paralysis: Being unable to move.

post-mortem: The medical examination of a corpse, to find out how and when a person died.

prosecution: The group of people who argue in court that someone is guilty of a crime.

remand: Being kept in prison until a trial.

safe: A metal box with a lock, where money or valuables are kept.

shoplifter: Someone who steals products from shops.

swab: A piece of soft material which can be used to take DNA samples, for example from the inside of the mouth.

toxicologist: An expert on poisons and poisoning.

young offender: A criminal who is not yet an adult.

Index